Books are to be returned on or before
the last date below.

ANG_____of

twent **2 0 JUN 2008** in
access **1 1 SEP 2008** b-
ject. I · le
book ; rs
in bib ɔy
Paulir ʋe
treatn us
being:

ADRI In
this b ly
togeth · ly
Christ a
textbc in
persec ld
teache

PAUI n
Scotla n
of woc n
these

ANGELS

Adrian Roberts

ANGELS

BY

ADRIAN ROBERTS

WOODCUTS BY

PAULINE JACOBSEN

THE CELTIC CROSS PRESS

ISBN 0 948261 65 X

Published by
Ovin Books
Ovins Well House
Lastingham
York YO62 6TJ

printed @maxiprint.co.uk

CONTENTS

New Testament

For my sons Theo and Hal

'Non Angli sed angeli'

INTRODUCTION

DO not mock those who believe in angels. Reality may be even more colourful and varied than you think. Down the ages many people in many cultures have seen and talked with beings believed to be from another world, who have brought messages of spiritual comfort or warning at critical moments. One of the grounds for rejecting supernatural events given by the philosopher David Hume was that they tend to be believed by illiterate and generally credulous people. It is true that some people do seem to show a natural inclination to believe in wonders, but this has nothing to do with their educational accomplishments. Hume had all the snobbery of an eighteenth century Edinburgh academic for cultures and classes he believed to be inferior, but these days we cannot afford to be so dismissive. Plenty of comparatively educated people take horoscopes seriously, and some even claim to have had dealings with aliens. The strange and various beliefs of the New Age movement have arisen in some of the world's most educated and technologically advanced regions. Conversely, there are some people, not necessarily the most educated, who will not believe anything unless it is staring them in the face.

What are angels anyway? Behind all the intricate classifications of the 5th century Greek monk and theologian Dionysius the Areopagite, it seems that they may be regarded as intermediaries between God and man: the word 'angel' means messenger in Greek, and that is as good a definition as any.

There is no point discussing the existence of angels except on the basis that there is a God, and a God who can communicate with us in history, not just a God who creates the universe and then loses interest. There is a logical order to debates. How many people have wasted time defending the historical evidence for the resurrection of Jesus, only to find that their opponent thinks that God is incapable of intervening in history in any event? If there is a God who takes an interest in his creatures, there is no reason to doubt that he may communicate with us in various ways. If there is a heaven, why not populate it with other creatures in addition to the souls of the blest? Look at the great and prodigal variety of species in the universe, of both plants and animals: God clearly loves diversity, and why not in heaven as much as on earth?

Angels may be defined quite simply, but their appearance is multiform. Someone might say, 'Yes, I believe in angels, but not as golden youths with feathery wings'. But that image of them is one among many: the depiction of angels like that has its own symbolism, and that is fine, so long as we do not limit ourselves to that depiction.

When people have met an angel it is often going to be difficult to record what it was like: it might have been in a dream or in some other altered state of consciousness. Sometimes it has seemed best to use stylised and symbolic imagery, particularly when the immediacy of the impression has been lost, or the account is an ancient one of uncertain significance. A golden youth may sometimes capture the impression, but equally it may be a monstrous beast, a cherub whose dimensions have been conjured up by the winged man-faced lions of Assyrian art. The armed cherubim at the gates of Eden share with the childlike cherubs of popular lore a certain innocence, but innocence does not have to be childlike: at the gates of Eden it is an innocence which is fierce and terrifyingly pure. The cherubim in the Garden of Eden are not messengers who bring comfort, but guards set to prevent the first people from returning to the paradise which they have forfeited by their disobedience.

Frequently angels appear like us: they are people we meet, and it only occurs to us later that there was something strange about the meeting. Abraham sits outside his tent, and three strangers come up: at first he assumes they are men like him: only in retrospect does it become clear that the encounter is a divine one.

Some angelic encounters in the Old Testament retain traces of an older set of beliefs, in which people were thought to have

2

walked and talked with God himself on earth: In Genesis God walks in the garden of Eden in the cool of the day. In this respect the stories about God dealing with humans face to face are much like the folklore of any ancient religion. However the Bible records a striking development: anthropomorphic conceptions of God come to be rejected. At first it seems that the sight of God is simply too much for feeble humans, though in Exodus Moses is offered a glimpse. Thereafter, God comes to be seen as pure spirit, whose form cannot be captured by any representation.

The Jews were unique in this belief, in their strict conception of blasphemy, and in their reluctance even to use God's name. But God was not relegated to a distant place where he could have no part in his creation. For a start, there were the old stories. But God's part in these comes to be taken by angels. Heaven is still communicating with earth, but now via beings who can take visible form. In some of the biblical texts as we have them, there are traces of these older versions: sometimes an angel seems to be speaking and sometimes God speaks. It is not always clear, for the angel's words are coming from God anyway.

Angels therefore develop a function as intermediaries. Of course, this is to simplify a more complex situation. The religiosity of the Bible as we know it emphasises an immaterial and transcendent God directing his heavenly court of angels. But we know that in ancient Israel polytheistic beliefs survived even after the revelation of one true God. This explains the anger shown by so many of the prophets, and for some people there must have been little to choose between angels and various lesser forms of deity.

Angels in their various shapes come and go at will. They may appear as humans, but there is nothing essential about this manifestation. As humans they are in disguise, and in the story of Tobias and the angel, the theme of disguise is vividly emphasised. Angels pass themselves off as particular individuals with assumed names. Their humanity is an illusion, no more part of their nature than a monstrous or animal appearance.

The coming of Jesus exploded all previous notions of communication between God and humanity. In the Old Testament God had given the Law to Moses and his Word to the prophets, and angels came to deliver immediate and urgent messages at critical points. To the earliest Christians, working as Jews within a biblical framework, it was clear that Jesus had a unique relationship with God. They also had clear memories of him as a man who lived among us; he was not a mythical figure from a distant past. So the gospels represent him as a new lawgiver and prophet operating on an unprecedented scale. But there are also traces of attempts to represent him as an angel, for like an angel he was a visible intermediary between God and the world, and like a heavenly being he could not be contained by the grave.

However, Jesus had gone lower than any previous angel; he had worked and suffered alongside us, he had loved and wept, he had cleansed the Temple in anger, unlike the angels who had calmly rained down fire on Sodom. His material humanity was not in doubt. And although he had descended this far, he had returned, and taken his material humanity with him to a state far higher than any angel's: true equality with God himself. The New Testament is a record of these ideas bursting into being in riotous profusion as the first few generations of Christians tried to make sense of what had happened. Any possible identification of Jesus as an angel was explicitly ruled out by the writer of Hebrews, who in passing starts a process of understanding the significance of angels in a Christian context.

For it might be thought that henceforth angels would be irrelevant. The coming of Jesus gradually made obsolete for Christians the work of law-giving and prophecy. Now that God had come to us in human form as his own mediator, what need was there for other beings to communicate his purposes? In the New Testament angelic visitations in which angels perform their basic function of bringing a message are mainly confined to the months before Jesus' birth: angels appear to Zechariah, to Mary, Joseph and the shepherds. Thereafter they reappear at the empty tomb and at the Ascension, to bring messages about Jesus when the mode of communication *with* Jesus is having to change. At these moments Jesus has withdrawn into a transcendence like God's. At the empty tomb he is encountered in his absence. (When he actually appears after his resurrection, there is no need for angelic attendants). At the Ascension he is no longer available to be encountered in the flesh, but the angels are needed to assure his followers that he will be with them in his spirit: they will not find him by looking up into the sky.

After the Ascension angels once more come into their own as servants of God, servants who do not challenge the uniqueness of Jesus' mediation, as the writer of Hebrews makes clear. They offer glimpses of the workings of heaven. In the Acts of the Apostles they release the apostles from prison in dream or vision-like experiences. In the book of Revelation they carry out the terrible purposes of God, they are guardians of the various churches, and they announce the end of the world. They are higher spirits, created by God at an earlier time, and like humans, some of them have fallen. This fall, unlike Adam's, does not infect the whole species, but it does spoil the world at its very start.

Christianity comes near to dualism in its contention that in a sense the world has been taken over by the devil and his angels, and that the power of God can only be shown by Jesus in the way of the cross and a disputed resurrection. Comes near to dualism, but not quite there: the fallen angels are creatures like us, and the war in heaven ends in their defeat, as Revelation makes clear, and the writer of Jude's letter imagines them in chains awaiting their own judgement.

This is a cosmic myth rather than a primeval event as imagined by Milton. The defeat of the devil is not an event predating or postdating the cross and resurrection, it is simply the effect that they have. The war in heaven is a mythological account of the work of Jesus. The figure of Jesus extends across both history and myth, and angels are relegated to a world of dreams, myths and visionary experiences.

And yet it would be a sad thing if the coming of Jesus robbed the heavens of their richness. Rather it brought them to fulfillment, and in the fulfilling the richness is contained, not cancelled out. Myths should not be defined as fanciful stories expressing some mundane truth. What is myth on earth may be fact in heaven. People continue to meet angels, and not always only in dreams. This may be an echo and hint of a universe of greater diversity and more varied reality than we are fully aware of in our limited existence.

Adrian Roberts Reformation Sunday 1996

GUARDIANS OF THE TREE OF LIFE

GENESIS ch3 v24

THE story of the garden of Eden may have been composed as early as the tenth century BC, and then set in a wider account of the world's creation as part of a priestly tradition of writings in the fifth century BC. The cherubim are fearsome creatures, nothing like the innocent 'cherubs' of later European art. Cherubim are pure and innocent, but innocence has no connection with childishness. The purity of the cherubim in this Genesis passage is indicated by the flaming sword.

The writers of the Old Testament are cruelly aware that man can never return to paradise, that realm of universal harmony. Contrary to some interpretations, Adam and Eve were not punished for disobeying an irrational command (refraining from one type of fruit amongst so many others) nor for discovering their sexuality, but for denying the truth of creation. They were given an authority delegated from the creator God and were to rule creation as representatives of God's loving power. Their attempt to seize the tree of knowledge (and if possible the tree of life) represents their desire to see themselves as acting on their own authority, to be, as the serpent put it, like God.

The irony of the situation was that they anyway reflected God's glory as created by him. Their attempt to go further involved them in the lie that they were more than creatures. God's sovereignty as creator could never be threatened, but the effect of the lie was a fundamental spoiling of several interlocking relationships: man with God, man with man, and man with nature. Thereafter humans are less aware of the presence of God. By eating meat they prey on other creatures, who themselves prey on each other. After Cain and Abel, murderous violence multiplies. Within the family the harmony between men and women breaks down: the woman cannot escape her need for the man to whom she is joined, but the relationship becomes one of submission. Childbirth, supposed to be joyful, becomes dangerous and agonising. Gathering food becomes a chore: the earth will not yield up its fruits unbidden, and man has to dig for his food at the mercy of the changing seasons.

The writers of this story have looked at all the unpleasant facts of life and found their cause in some primordial breakdown in the relationship between humans and God. They believed that God had created everything good: the breakdown was the responsibility of man. Evil results. Suffering is not introduced by God, but is brought about by man. God's last act before expelling Adam and Eve from the garden is one of love, and is earthy and intimate. One effect of the fall is sexual shame, so '*the Lord made for Adam and for his wife garments of skins, and clothed them*'.

The expulsion from the garden was not then so much a punishment as the result of a disordered condition introduced by man. For a creature to pretend to be his own creator involves an absurdity: paradise is destroyed, and thereafter humans lose sight of God. Though they grow more violent they in fact become weaker (hence the shorter lifespans as the Old Testament progresses).

The power of this story is universal. Although none of us have ever lived in Eden, we can share a sense of loss, an ache and yearning to return. The world we now live in is beautiful but predatory and changeable. All grace, nobility and loveliness are liable to decay and corruption. Love and friendship bring us joy, but then grow cold. We know the delight of sexual love, the desire to unite ourselves with another person for life, but we know too the pain and shame of broken hearts and promises. Something has been lost, otherwise we would not feel its absence. The prophets knew this sense of loss, and looked for a time when disharmony, disability, disease, and the cruelty of the natural world would come to an end. Glimpses of this hope punctuate the narrative of the rest of the Old Testament, that sadly realistic record of faithlessness, failure, and the enduring patience of God.

The cherubim barring the way to paradise symbolise a frontier which man can no longer cross. They are also a protection: were man to be allowed to continue to abuse his authority as guardian of paradise, the devastation wrought by him would be that much more terrible. The way back to God is long and hard, and as a sign that God has not taken back his love, angels thereafter are occasionally sent to guide and admonish, but also to bring messages of promise and comfort.

HAGAR IN THE DESERT

GENESIS ch16 vv1-16

THIS story is a haunting digression from the main theme of this section of Genesis, which is the covenant made by God with Abraham. Ten years have passed since God has promised in-numerable descendants to Abraham, and yet he is still without a son. Sarah offers to Abraham her Egyptian maidservant Hagar, in the hope that she will bear him a son on Sarah's behalf. (This practice is found authorised in a Hurrian code of law dating from the fifteenth century BC: the barren wife would bring up the maidservant's child as her own). Hagar bears a son, and begins to regard Sarah with contempt. Sarah treats her badly, and Hagar flees into the desert. There the angel of the Lord meets her and tells her to return to her mistress. He brings from God the promise that her son, Ishmael, although destined to be a wild and solitary man, will be the father of many descendants. The angel uses language reminiscent of the promise of descendants given to Abraham in the previous chapter. It is clear that the main line of God's promise is not due to descend through Ishmael (the chosen son Isaac will be born to Sarah in chapter 21, and once more Hagar returns to the desert, this time dismissed by Sarah and accompanied by Ishmael). But in both chapters 16 and 21 the angel of the Lord brings Hagar words of comfort and promise: the child is still Abraham's and will be cherished by God.

There are many elements of interest here. The angel is simply a messenger relaying the words of God. He is not given a name or any defining characteristics as he might be in a later tradition. In the version of the story here he represents the belief that since no one can face God directly, communication with God must take place through intermediaries. This is a function of angels in the finished versions of many stories of divine encounters in the Old Testament. However, there is an intriguing echo of an earlier version of the Hagar story at 16:13, where Hagar seems to think that she has seen God himself: in some translations of the Hebrew she is surprised that she is still alive. God is depicted as caring for the afflicted, but this is also an aetiological tale describing the origin of the Arabs of the desert, the Ishmaelites. The writers are aware that God does not care only for Israel: he has made a covenant in similar terms with despised and violent marauding tribesmen (for so the Ishmaelites were regarded). Israel was the chosen people, but God had a plan for gentile nations as well. This enlightened 'universalist' attitude is also found in parts of Isaiah.

The text of parts of this story is corrupt, and the translation uncertain. Two variants soften the harshness of the story as often told: Hagar does not actually treat Sarah with contempt - her fertility is, understandably in the culture of the time, itself a reproach to Sarah - and the Ishmaelites are not necessarily to be understood as living in permanent hostility towards their Israelite kinsmen: the text could simply mean they will live as nomads on the borders of Israel. Modern ignorance has lent a romance to the tale which is absent from the original. When she leaves Sarah, Hagar does not wander aimlessly in the desert, but takes the desert road to Shur, the most direct route back to Egypt, her country of origin.

ABRAHAM AND THE THREE MEN

GENESIS ch18 vv1-16

THIS passage is considered one of the masterpieces of Hebrew story telling. Once again it is not clear whether Abraham encounters God himself or merely three of his angels: it is possible that one of the three men is supposed to be God himself, for thereafter the two others, clearly designated angels, go on to destroy Sodom and Gomorrah. The fathers of the early church thought that the three men represented the Trinity.

The atmosphere of this scene is well drawn. Abraham is dozing in the middle of the day and is woken by three strangers striding towards him. Abraham is clearly aware that these are no ordinary men - it is not made clear why - and they stand in commanding silence while he bustles round preparing refreshment for them. Their words are simple and authoritative, and they repeat the promise of God that Abraham and Sarah will have a son, not at some unspecified time in the future, but soon. Powerful contrasts are drawn here: the scene is a homely one, the hospitable nomad entertains his guests. But there is an air of mystery: the strangers may look like men, but one of them may be God himself, and the others are about to go off and destroy two major cities. Sarah is rebuked for doubting the promise, but there is no threat of punishment (contrast the treatment of Zechariah in Luke's gospel). The writer may be intentionally depicting God as at once close and distant, transcendent in his authority but also able to have an intimate relationship with one of his creatures. This would explain why the atmosphere veers between the very human and mundane on the one hand and the strange and numinous on the other.

'Do not neglect to show hospitality to strangers, for thereby some have entertained angels unawares'. The anonymous writer of the letter to Hebrews is probably thinking of this story amongst others. Abraham's spontaneous welcome to the three men is an important element in the story. The promise of a son is not a reward for hospitality shown, for it is already part of God's plan before the angels arrive, but Abraham's behaviour is all part of the fact that he has already been chosen by God as the recipient of the great promise of descendants and land, and has already responded in faith. The cities of Sodom and Gomorrah provide a dramatic contrast. They are marked out for destruction because of their sinfulness (sexual sins are not initially specified but presumably included), and their response to the arrival of the three angels is to attempt to subject them to a homosexual rape. Apart from anything else, this is a gross breach of hospitality, and the fact that the angels do not identify themselves puts the story into the tradition mentioned in Hebrews: not even the inhabitants of Sodom would have been foolish enough to try indecent assault on the angel of the Lord had he actually announced himself as such.

The Jews were not the only ones to imagine the testing effect on a household of divine or angelic guests arriving in disguise. In the Greek story of Baucis and Philemon, a version of the flood myth, the gods Zeus and Hermes travel the world in disguise, but find no welcome among the rich: only Baucis and Philemon, a poor couple, will entertain them. As a reward they are saved from the flood which soon engulfs the world, and as the first priest and priestess re-establish religion.

Many people these days have stories to tell of encounters with angels, in which the angel is usually in disguise and only recognised as such in retrospect, in virtue of help or advice brought in such a way as can hardly be coincidence. In fact to talk of disguise at all is perhaps inappropriate: we are not yet twenty chapters into Genesis and it is already clear that angels are defined not by any particular appearance, but by their function as mediators between God and man.

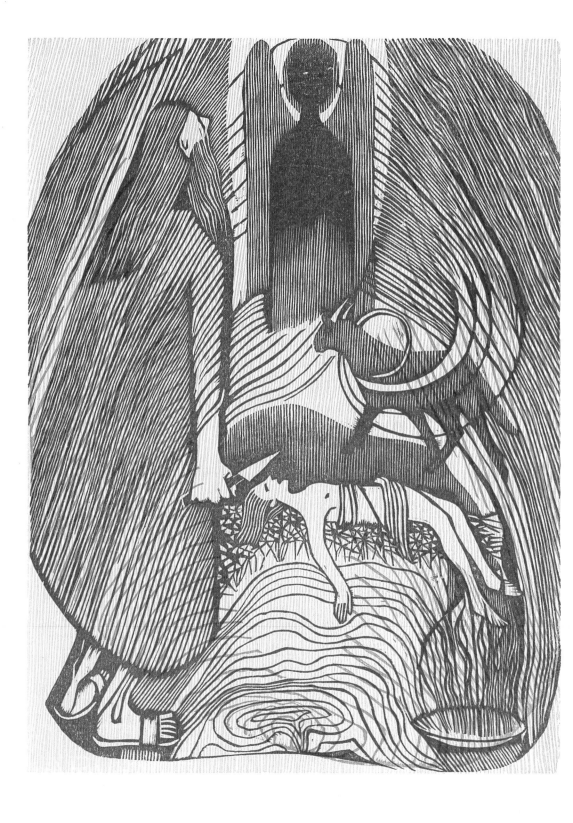

ABRAHAM AND ISAAC

GENESIS ch22 vv11-18

IN this terrible story of faith put to the test God requires from Abraham the ultimate act of obedience: he is to sacrifice his only son, the son given to him after many years of childlessness.

As the story unfolds there is no hint of final remission. The command comes directly from God, and Abraham has to travel with his son to the place of sacrifice without giving the boy any indication of his purpose. The reader is left to imagine Abraham's pain as he prepares to carry out the instructions. Isaac is puzzled and confused about the apparent lack of a sacrificial victim, and Abraham, a man of faith, replies, '*God will provide the lamb.*' There is a note of desperate trust in his words, and as he raises his hand to slay his son someone reading this passage for the first time might be prepared for a tragic conclusion. But at this final moment the voice of the angel of the Lord from heaven stays his hand with the marvellous words of comfort, '*Abraham, Abraham… do not lay your hand on the lad or do anything to him.*' A ram is provided, Abraham's trust is vindicated, and the story ends quickly with an account of animal sacrifice, the site being given a name of sacred significance.

It is interesting that whereas the original command comes from God himself, the words of comfort ending the horror are mediated through an angel. Yet the story may be understood on one level as a condemnation of human sacrifice, a practice which seems to have occurred at ancient Canaanite shrines and which was denounced by the prophets as a pagan practice occasionally resorted to by the more wicked kings of Israel. At another level, it may preserve a memory of a time when the ancestors of the Israelites themselves

17

thought that God really did require human offerings. After all, the laws of Exodus make it clear that first born children belong to God in a special way, but may be redeemed by specified rituals. In this story the command is tied into Abraham's covenant of faith, in which he has to be prepared to give up everything including his son, to receive it back as a gracious gift from God. Through his angel God restores the bond between father and son and provides an animal as an acceptable sacrifice, restoring the covenant relationship in which God does not take back his gift.

The mount of Moriah where the sacrifice takes place has not been identified. There is a tradition that it was the site of the Temple Mount in Jerusalem, later the central and finally the only place of sacrifice for the Jews. For the Christian Fathers, anxious perhaps to mitigate the cruelty of the original story, Isaac represented Jesus, the only begotten Son of God, whose sacrificial death emptied all previous cults of significance and was itself swallowed up in resurrection. In a pessimistic modern retelling of the story, Abraham disobeys the angel and kills his son, thus representing the generation of elderly politicians who plunged Europe into the First World War, sacrificing a generation of young men in the trenches of Flanders. But this treatment destroys the positive denouement of the biblical version in which the sombre atmosphere of the story is overcome by the joyful and triumphant words of the angel releasing Abraham from his bond and reaffirming the terms of God's covenant with his people.

MOSES AND THE BURNING BUSH

EXODUS ch3 v2

MOSES is in exile in the land of Midian after having murdered an Egyptian. At this low point in his fortunes he comes across a marvellous sight: a bush burning without being consumed. We are told that the angel of the Lord appears to him from the bush, but the voice which comes from it is the voice of God. The scene begins with an apparently chance encounter: Moses sees the strange phenomenon and goes closer out of his route to investigate. Thus begins an experience which changes the rest of his life. God identifies himself by the name of Yahweh, and says he is the same God who was worshipped under various names by Abraham, Isaac and Jacob. He reveals his fundamental nature as a God who has adopted the Hebrews and pitied their sufferings in Egypt, and he promises to deliver them and give them a new land. In this way the covenant made with Abraham is now extended to his descendants, who are to be turned by God into a great nation.

Why does God speak to Moses from a bush? This is no angelic visitation in human form. The idea of an unconsumed burning bush may be derived from an ancient awareness that petroleum deposits on a bush can ignite without burning the bush itself, but it is foolish to suppose that Moses had simply misunderstood a natural phenomenon, for this would not explain the voice. The writers may simply be borrowing from natural experience to describe the indescribable, an encounter with God himself. Fire is a common and understandable biblical image for the presence of God (angels are frequently said to be bright and fiery in appearance). Fire destroys, purifies and brings light and warmth. The fire which does

not consume the bush is appropriately enough a divine fire because it behaves in an unusual way. Moses is warned to take off his shoes and to keep his distance in the presence of the divine, and he cannot look directly at the bush. No one can see God and live, but of all men, on several occasions, Moses, the chosen one, comes closest to a direct vision of God.

This part of Exodus contains an enormous shift in the Israelite understanding of God, and the meeting of various traditions. The patriarchs worshipped a God who stayed with them in their wanderings. Yahweh, the God encountered by Moses, may originally have been understood as a local god of Midian, the area around Sinai/Horeb. It is there that Moses meets him in the burning bush, and later Sinai is the first destination for the Israelites when they leave Egypt after telling Pharaoh that they wished to worship God there. But he turns out to be no mere local deity. His name Yahweh is mysterious, a refusal to give a designating and limiting name, being interpreted as something like 'I am the one who is'. And so, like the patriarchs, the wandering Israelites can continue to worship Yahweh as he accompanies them through the desert, represented in angelic form by pillars of cloud and fire. He adopts the people of Israel, and becomes their God wherever they are, and as time goes on he comes to be understood as the greatest and indeed the only God of all.

Human figures, animals, flaming bushes and voices. The Old Testament has no single way of representing angels, but through all the stories comes the clear indication that to encounter an angel is somehow to be in the presence of God himself.

THE ANGEL AS GUARD

EXODUS ch23 v20

THE verses preceding this promise are a list of legal requirements to be imposed on the Israelites during their occupation of the promised land. These laws are characterised by a concern for the vulnerable, and the demand that one may not abuse a position of advantage to destroy a personal enemy. It is impossible to read them without a sense of admiration for the people who composed them, seeing as they did to the heart of what destroys or makes any society. The laws range from the solemn to the mundane: no false witness, but also, if you find your enemy's ox going astray, return it. There is particular concern for slaves and aliens, and when it comes to sabbath keeping, the lawmakers seem to be thinking of social justice as much as of sacred days: employees need a day of rest and will not get one unless it is imposed by law. The Israelites must always remember that they too were once slaves: the call to sympathise with others on the basis of a common experience shows the humane warmth of these laws.

There is no advantage to be expected from keeping them, in fact they seem to rule out any self interest. But verse 20 introduces the promise that the Israelites are to be given an angel to guide them into the promised land, and it is made clear that the angel's protection is dependent upon obedience to his word.

Although the angel may command obedience on God's behalf, he is clearly to be understood as a being separate from God, a proper intermediary. This verse is the first known introduction of the idea of guardian angels. Guardian angels can be attached to nations (as here), to individuals (as later, in the book of Tobit), and even to churches, as in the book of Revelation. As an idea they are at the very least a way to express a feeling of divine protection or of a demanding divine challenge: guardian angels admonish as well as protect.

And yet the angel here, while not to be confused with God himself, shows how close God can come to dwelling with his people, the holy and transcendent one sanctifying a sinful and wandering nation. The angel may be represented as bearing the divine name, as accompanying the people as cloud or fire, or as associated with the ark of the covenant. All these are concrete and visible manifestations of a Godhead understood from an early date as being in himself invisible and not to be captured by any human representation.

On the other hand, it would be anachronistic to suppose that God was conceived of as being transcendent in a modern abstract sense, as a sort of "God of the philosophers", logically distinct from the universe, and showing at best very faint signs of his power. The biblical texts as we have them preserve a sense of the presence of God, both when angels are involved and when they are not. The language used for God's presence is not *simply* literal, but it is not *simply* metaphorical either. The impression we get is of great variety in imagery and expression. Pagan gods are rejected, not because they do not exist (a very modern objection to them), but because they are less effective and worthy of worship than is the God of Israel. They need temples to live in, and are limited by the contours of a statue. The God of Israel came to have a temple, but it was only his "name" which dwelt there, and an empty throne. Statues and images there may have been, but of mythical beasts, not of God himself. It was not that he dwelt outside the boundaries of the universe, but that the temple, and the world of limited experience, were too small to contain him. He could be encountered on mountains in wind and fire, he could even occasionally be seen, though the experience might kill you. He went before his people in the wilderness: the wind and fire were only signs of his presence, but the signs were real, and the presence was felt.

The blessings brought by the angel are earthly and concrete ones: conquest and slaughter of one's enemies, followed by a long and happy life as one dwells secure in the land and leaves it to one's children. Disobedience, on the other hand, will bring defeat and disaster. The Jews who read this passage knew that although their ancestors had indeed won a land, they had also gone on to suffer defeat and a series of disasters. Tradition also told how a long line of corrupt kings and religious leaders had led the people astray and lost God's active support. The picture was clear: God originally brought himself to their notice by his deeds of dramatic rescue, the parting of the waves, the provision of food and water in the desert, and the destruction of the kingdoms of Canaan. Much of this Israelite faith was hardly 'spiritual' in any modern sense at all. Then bitter experience taught a difficult and ultimately more profound lesson: God's holiness might not be vindicated in any concrete fashion, perhaps not even in this life at all. In spite of the natural human desire for neat explanations it turned out that Israel suffered disasters even when she was being loyal to God, and conversely, that even in her times of disobedience God remained true to his adoption of her. So it came to be realised that God's holiness and love involve a limitless capacity for forgiveness and that his promise can only be fulfilled in another world altogether.

BALAAM AND THE ASS

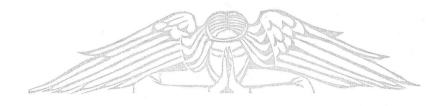

NUMBERS ch22 vv22-25

AS it stands, the text of this incident is muddled, or else the inconsistencies have been deliberately worked into it to make some subtle point.

The context is the Israelite conquest of Canaan. The Israelites are enjoying great success, so the Moabites and Midianites send a message to Balaam, a seer who lives by the river Euphrates, asking him to come to their territories and curse the Israelites. Warned by God that the Israelites have the divine blessing, Balaam refuses to go back with the envoys: more powerful envoys are sent, and at this point Balaam is told by God that he should accompany them after all, and await further instructions. He sets off with his donkey, and we are told that God is angry at this; the angel of the Lord with a drawn sword blocks his path. Unfortunately, only the donkey can see the angel, and it tries several times to turn from the road. The bewildered Balaam is annoyed and beats the animal, until God opens its mouth and it rebukes Balaam, pointing out that it has hitherto served him faithfully. Only then does God allow Balaam to see the angel. Balaam apologises for his ignorance and offers to go home, but the angel sends him on with his journey, reiterating God's command that when he reaches his destination he is only to say what God tells him to say.

It may be that there were originally two versions of the story; in one Balaam sides with Israel and in the other he sides with her enemies. Otherwise one can imagine Balaam is simply failing to pick up the changing nuances of God's commands: his eyes and ears are not sufficiently open to the divine. He blunders ahead and it is

27

only his humble donkey who notices the presence of the angel standing before them. The lowly beast of burden gets the message missed by the wise seer.

The angel with the drawn sword reminds us of the cherubim at the gates of Eden. In that story too there is a talking animal, the serpent, and the rarity of this motif has suggested to some that the two stories come from the same tradition. However, as Jewish (and later Christian) tradition developed, the serpent came to be identified with the devil: Balaam's ass is the only true talking animal as such in the Bible. The incident of the encounter between ass and angel is thus all the more memorable and striking. A normally dumb animal making a prophetic utterance, and then returning to speechlessness produces a startling effect. There are no talking animals in Homer's Iliad, for example, except in one scene where the chariot horses of Achilles are temporarily given the power of speech by the gods, and prophesy their master's death.

THE ANGEL AND THE PLAGUE

2 SAMUEL ch24 vv15-25

ANGEL as destroyer: a new idea is introduced in the second book of Samuel. We have seen angels coming to comfort and warn, to rebuke and to bar the way, but even at Sodom the actual destruction was wrought by the hand of God. But here we see an angel smiting God's own people with plague.

The context is that king David has taken a census of his people. God has incited him to do this, but it is a sinful thing to do. The text implies that God's motive is to give himself an excuse for punishing Israel, but we are not told why he is angry in the first place. The explanation may be that God's incitement is like his hardening of Pharaoh's heart: the writer is indicating his own belief that even evil actions are somehow under God's all-encompassing authority. As a result of the census God asks David to choose one amongst famine, military defeat and plague as his punishment: he chooses plague, as being a punishment most clearly coming from God himself. Seventy thousand die, but when the angel of the Lord stretches out his hand to destroy Jerusalem, God stops him: '*It is enough. Now stay your hand*'. The angel has been standing outside the city, at the threshing floor of Araunah the Jebusite. (Jebusites were the original Canaanite inhabitants of Jerusalem). David buys the threshing floor and builds an altar there to offer sacrifices of expiation. It was later included within the city boundary and is believed to have been the site of Solomon's Temple.

The story is both interesting and confusing: two separate themes may have coalesced, in one of which the plague is stopped by God's compassionate initiative, and in the other of which it is David's intercessory prayer which does the trick. It was certainly believed that there was something blasphemous about taking a census. You seek to number your people accurately to try to gain and exercise a centralised control, but the people belong to God, and as king you are at most God's deputy. There is a strong anti-monarchist strain running through parts of the books of Samuel, indicated by the repeated claim that God is the only king, and by Samuel's warning that asking for an earthly king was inviting oppression: censuses were used to facilitate taxation, forced labour and military service. Yet the king was God's anointed. The ambiguity is well reflected in this story: the plague happens, but David gets away with it.

The angel who inflicts the plague is not identified except as being an angel of the Lord. In 2 Kings 19 he slaughters the army of Sennacherib the Assyrian as it besieges Jerusalem: no manner of death is mentioned, but again, plague may be suspected. As time went on destruction came to be associated not with the angel of the Lord, but with an angel of death and destruction. This is the angel named by the book of Revelation, Abaddon, or in Greek, Apollyon, the angel of the bottomless pit. In the vision he leads the army of locusts to torment the inhabitants of the earth for a time. He is not Satan, the fallen angel, but an instrument of God's wrath. His name means the Destroyer (Apollyon comes from the Greek verb 'to destroy'). Some ancient scholars used to link the name of Apollo, the god of healing, with this verb. In the Iliad he punishes the Greek army by shooting them with his invisible arrows (ie pestilence). He was sometimes called the mouse god, and some have thought that this is a reference to plague-bearing rodents. The Greek historian Herodotus tells a story about Sennacherib in which an invasion against Egypt fails because mice eat through the Assyrian bow strings as the army lies encamped. Is this a variant version of the story in 2 Kings? Pagan beliefs about a Greek god Apollo and Jewish ones about a destroying angel called Abaddon/Apollyon may have been intertwined at a time before any of these stories came to be written down.

ELIJAH'S FLIGHT FROM JEZEBEL

1 KINGS ch19 vv5-8

THE angelic encounter here marks a crisis or turning point in the fortunes of the prophet Elijah. The story so far: Ahab, king of the northern kingdom of Israel, has married a pagan princess, Jezebel, who has introduced the worship of Baal to Israel along with a cadre of pagan prophets. The worship of Baal becomes very popular with the Israelites, provoking Elijah to organise a trial of strength between Baal and Yahweh. There follows the famous fire-raising contest, as Elijah calls down the fire of God onto his soaking altar, and then leads a massacre of the unsuccessful prophets of Baal.

But this victory is by no means the end of the story. Jezebel threatens revenge, and Elijah flees to Beersheba in the southern kingdom of Judah, where he leaves his servant and treks on into the wilderness until he collapses under a broom tree and prays for death. His words suggest a state of mind bordering on despair: '*It is enough; now, O Lord, take away my life, for I am no better than my fathers.*'

Gone is any sense of triumph in his recent victory and the restoration of right worship in Israel. Instead Elijah has lost his way both physically and in his heart: travelling aimlessly through a desert, apparently without food or water, his only destination is death. He has achieved nothing and he is nothing, '*I am no better than my fathers.*' He falls asleep.

What wakes him is an angel's touch, and the command to rise and eat. There is no vision, but Elijah gets up to find that food and water have been provided for him: he goes back to sleep, and wakes to a second angelic command to refresh himself with more food and

drink which again have been provided *'else the journey will be too great for you.'*

Restored and strengthened, Elijah travels forty days and nights until he reaches Horeb, the mountain of God. Was that then his destination all along, and was he fed by the angel simply because he had run out of food? Maybe so, but the writer makes no mention of Elijah actually needing to eat, or of Horeb as his destination, until the angel appears. Up to that point, harried by his enemies, he wanders into the desert and asks to die. The angel shakes him out of his depression by ordering him to eat of the food set before him, and by giving a point to his journey, the mountain of God. The food sustains Elijah for the symbolic period of forty days and nights (*cf* the forty years in the wilderness) and on Horeb he encounters God in a cave. He tells God of Israel's betrayal, and of his own zeal for God and consequent danger. His tone is confident: his trust in God (and in his own prophetic calling) seem to have been restored.

Horeb is the same as Sinai, the mountain where God revealed himself to Moses. God speaks to Elijah twice, and in the second encounter he appears not in the traditional media of wind, earthquake and fire, but in the still small voice. This new form of theophany is suitable for a prophet, who receives the word of God quietly in his heart, and Elijah is commanded to return to the prophetic functions of proclaiming judgement and anointing kings, and indeed his own successor, Elisha.

At his lowest point, then, Elijah is touched by an angel and raised to the level of Moses: just as Moses brought Israel to worship Yahweh the true God, so Elijah brings the northern kingdom back to him by the angel's hand. Tradition had it that Elijah did not die, but was taken to heaven while still living. Many expected that he would return to inaugurate the messianic age, and he appears with Moses and Jesus in the gospel vision of the Transfiguration.

RAPHAEL AND TOBIAS

TOBIT ch5 vv5-28

WITH the book of Tobit we are in the realm of romance. It contains several folk motifs: the successful quest, the grateful dead, the monster in the bridal chamber, and the angelic companion in disguise, firmly named here by the narrator as Raphael, whose name means '*God heals*'.

Tobit is a comparatively late work, around 200BC, but its dramatic date is the depopulation of the northern kingdom of Israel from 722BC: Tobit and his family are Israelites in exile at Nineveh, and his son's journey takes him to Ecbatana in Media. Historical and geographical details are unimportant and so inaccuracies are to be expected, for the author tackles some important moral themes: we are tested, not punished by God in our sufferings, and we must continue to strive to reflect God's justice and freedom in our own lives, in the sure hope that eventually, but still in this present life, virtue and wickedness will receive their reward. Tobit and his family stand in the strict and exclusivist tradition of the Jewish law (foreign marriages are not recommended), but women play a positive and important role, whether earning money or composing prayers.

The background to the tale is double affliction: Tobit blinded in the course of piously burying the dead, and the loss to his distant kinswoman Sarah of seven husbands, each killed on his wedding night by the demon Asmodeus (Persian Aeshma Daeva, demon of wrath). Both Tobit and Sarah separately pray for help, and the angel Raphael is sent to bring about the restoration of their fortunes: he inspires Tobit to send his son Tobias on an errand to

Media (where Sarah lives) and the angel appears in disguise to accompany the lad. The narrator always refers to the angel as Raphael, but the characters in the story think he is Tobit's cousin Azariah (*'Yahweh has helped'*) son of Hananiah (*'Yahweh is merciful'*): the opportunities for dramatic irony are explored to the full, and Raphael reveals his identity only at the end. Tobit's wife Anna is worried about her son's plans to travel to Media: Tobit reassures her by saying that his angel will be there to guide him: little does he know that his words are literally true.

Raphael is in fact rather like a guardian angel, and this story is one of the sources for the widespread folk belief in guardian angels. He is also like the genie or divine guide in many traditional quest stories. Sarah's previous seven husbands have been killed in their ignorance by the demon Asmodeus who jealously haunts the bridal chamber. It is made clear from the start that Tobias is the one chosen to succeed, the one who is destined to have Sarah for his wife. Like all successful questers he is given privileged information by the divine guide, in this case the fact that the problem is caused by a demon, and that it can be chased away by smoking it out with a fire of incense on which the heart and liver of a fish have been laid. The gall bladder from the same fish is later used to anoint Tobit's eyes and so cure his blindness.

So Tobit is cured and Tobias marries Sarah. Raphael reveals himself, and both father and son fall on their faces in fear. Raphael's explanation tells us that the writer of Tobit is coming from a tradition which has begun to reflect deeply about what angels actually are, and what is their exact relation to man and God. Raphael points out that he has not eaten anything during the course of the journey, and this is because he has in fact been present only as a vision. It is perhaps best to end with the resounding words by means of which he announces himself, words which indicate an increasing interest on the part of the writer in angelic status and classification: *'I am Raphael, one of the seven holy angels who present the prayers of the saints and enter into the presence of the glory of the Holy One.'*

GABRIEL GIVES DANIEL UNDERSTANDING

DANIEL ch9 vv20-27

THE book of Daniel is set during the Jewish exile in Babylon (from 586BC), and tells of the hero Daniel's commitment to Jewish laws in a time of persecution. The book is not historical in the strict sense. The reigning Babylonian king is Belshazzar son of Nebuchadnezzar: in fact he was the son of Nabonidus, and never reigned as king. Cyrus the Persian is known as founder of a great empire, but Darius the Mede is otherwise quite unknown (though we know of later kings called Darius). Daniel himself belongs to the distant past: Ezekiel mentions him in connection with Noah and Job, and he appears in Ras Shamra texts of the 14th century BC. The book was probably written between 167 and 164BC, when the Jews were being persecuted again, this time by king Antiochus Epiphanes, descendant of one of those generals of Alexander the Great who had shared out his empire after his early death in 323BC. Antiochus had tried to impose Greek customs on the Jews, and the readers of this book are no doubt meant to be comforted by a story from the past of successful Jewish resistance to an earlier persecuting king.

Experience of foreign oppression called forth from Jewish writers a genre known as apocalyptic. Apocalyptic is characterised by exotic visions, angelic visitations, and coded messages promising a final dramatic vindication of God's purposes and a full understanding of his plans for human history. Daniel contains many apocalyptic elements.

Like Tobit, Daniel reflects a developed doctrine of angels: here

the angel is Gabriel (*'God is my warrior'*) who comes to teach Daniel understanding of the secret messages of God. There is a problem in the text here, for Daniel has just been praying for the sins of his people, not asking for understanding, and some think that two separate themes have coalesced. However, the understanding is given in the context of the atonement for sin, so perhaps there is a connection. Gabriel is represented as flying down to address Daniel, and it is important to appreciate that the depiction of angels as having wings has always been part of angelic imagery and never part of central angelic doctrine. Visions frequently involve winged creatures, and this is an appropriate part of the basic metaphor that God's realm is up in heaven, and that heavenly beings come down to earth. It is very unlikely that the sophisticated thinkers who wrote apocalyptic literature thought that God actually lives in the sky.

Gabriel comes to bring understanding, but the context of his explanation is no less obscure and enigmatic than anything else in the book. Apocalyptic never delivers an explanation intended to be clear and obvious to everyone: you have to be initiated, one of the elect whom God is going to save. This feeling of having access to secret knowledge must have been very important to people living under hostile regimes. However, one clear theme which recurs throughout Daniel is that of a human figure who will appear at the end of history to restore God's rule to the world: Daniel 7 contains the famous Son of Man vision, and Gabriel even mentions in an oblique way an anointed prince or messiah who will come to Jerusalem for a specified time.

It is appropriate to end here our selection of Old Testament texts, for we now come to the great revelation of the anointed king Jesus who will finally bridge once and for all the gulf between God and man, and so gather up and fulfill all previous angelic visitations. But angels continue to have a function, albeit more limited, and they appear at significant moments in the New Testament, and it is Gabriel who features in the early chapters of Matthew and Luke, to bring God's enlightenment and understanding to the puzzled and frightened parents of both John the Baptist and Jesus.

THE ANNUNCIATION

LUKE ch1 vv26-38

WE come to one of the most famous angelic visitations of all. It has been subject to many representations, from old masters to films. Sometimes Mary is a finely dressed maiden kneeling amongst colonnades and attended by a glorious Gabriel with rainbow wings, while more recent versions tend to favour Mary as a peasant girl in a hut and the angel as a shaft of light invisibly enlightening her mind. Is this second, more modern kind of representation any more 'realistic' than the traditional, as might be supposed? In fact surely both are unable to capture the full truth of the original event, which was the catalyst of the Incarnation, and therefore may be understood as a meeting between earth and heaven, of temporal and eternal, and limited human imagination will only be able to express a few facets at the expense of others.

And yet in Luke's account the Annunciation takes the form of something as easy to grasp and mundane as a conversation. Gabriel is once again performing his Old Testament role of the one who explains the purposes of God. Mary too stands in the role of the chosen human, bewildered and uncertain. With her, God's purposes take a new turn. In the Old Testament, and indeed earlier in Luke's gospel, the birth of a special child is promised to old and barren women: Sarah, Hannah, Elizabeth. But Luke remembers that Mary was young and unmarried at the time of Jesus' birth, and so the believer is asked to choose in faith between two possibilities: either there had been sexual infidelity, or else in the birth of Jesus God was going beyond the miraculous births of the Old Testament: here the greatest prophet of all, the final revelation of the word of

God, is born by a greater miracle to a young virgin.

This new pattern contained a hidden danger. The Greek god Zeus also used to visit young girls in disguise, and impregnate them with heroic children: what is the difference here? Zeus visited Danae as a shower of gold, and mediaeval thinkers used to say that the virginal conception of Jesus was a bit like a shaft of sunlight passing through a pane of glass which is left intact. It is important to notice that at the Annunciation nothing actually happens. There is simply a conversation between Mary and the angel. There is no imagery of congress or penetration, divine or otherwise. This is not because sexuality is in itself any more flawed than any other part of humanity, but because in the Annunciation Gabriel is heralding a unique bypassing of normal sexuality: sexual procreation is the human way of reflecting God's creativity. At the conception of Jesus this human reflection, and all images of it, must stand aside, because the birth of Jesus is to be a new beginning, a new reaching down of heaven to earth. Neither God himself, nor Gabriel as his agent, is replacing Joseph as one male may replace another in the sexual union, because neither God nor Gabriel is male in that sense at all.

Mary differs too from the recipients of angelic proclamation in the Old Testament, in that although she questions the angel closely she does not respond in mockery or disbelief. In the old stories there is some humour as the affronted angel is asked to prove himself. With Mary there is a reaction of complete trust and obedience to God: 'Let it be according to your word'. In this way she becomes the model and prototype of Christian discipleship.

THE CONCEPTION OF JESUS

MATTHEW ch1 vv18-25

AS in Luke, in Matthew also an angel announces the virginal conception of Jesus, but there are significant differences between the two accounts. Here the announcement is made to Joseph, thus prompting the theory that Matthew tells the story from Joseph's angle and Luke from Mary's. Matthew does not name his angel but goes back to an earlier Old Testament practice of attributing angelic appearances to an 'angel of the Lord'. Luke, echoing the late book of Daniel, calls attention to Gabriel as one who brings understanding. He says that Mary thought deeply about her experiences as Jesus grew up, and that Jesus himself grew in wisdom. Such sacred enlightenment is a feature of some of the later books of the Old Testament. Matthew is echoing a more ancient tradition deriving from the book of Exodus in which the angel of the Lord brings a reassurance of God's love and presence. Here Joseph is reassured, and the narrator's tone is confident: '...*she was found to be with child of the Holy Spirit*'.

Jesus is a descendant of David. The genealogy at the beginning of the gospel may not be strictly accurate, or even intended to be so, but there may have been a genuine family tradition of descent from Israel's greatest king. The angel addresses Joseph as son of David. It is interesting that the angel appears to Joseph in a dream. It was rare but not unknown in Jewish tradition for God to make known his purposes in dreams (see Sirach 34:1 for example). The angel refutes the slander that Jesus was illegitimate. Later writings made this suggestion, and Matthew may have been aware of it. Whether we think that Jesus is illegitimate, or conceived by God, it is important that Joseph, David's descendant, acknowledges him formally as his son. As God's anointed, David was the first Messiah, and the hopes which David generated will come to fruition in Jesus, though in a surprising way, not through victory and empire but through a love which conquers death. With this acknowledgement, Joseph must pass into the background. Mary stands for the Christian disciple who accepts the will of God. Joseph, the carpenter, the human craftsman, stands aside to allow God's direct creative activity to bring Jesus to birth. As God himself comes to earth in the wonder of incarnation, Mary receives him while Joseph stands back: Joseph stands for humanity given creative power by God, both as craftsman and, in normal circumstances, as a parent. On this one occasion he must do nothing but accept the angel's reassurance that the child comes from God.

And so we come to the proof text for the virgin birth as Matthew quotes Isaiah 7:14. It has given rise to debate: the Hebrew text specifies 'young woman' rather than virgin, the Greek text uses a word that indicates a virgin, and it has been supposed that the early Christians invented the doctrine of the virgin birth on the basis of a mistranslation, for they certainly used a Greek version of the Old Testament. It is more likely that there was a memory that Mary had been unmarried at the time of Jesus' birth. We are back to the choice: illegitimacy or an act of God. As a Christian, Matthew will have believed that Jesus' birth was from God. It was therefore appropriate for him to find a text to support what he already believed, and to find new meaning in it. What Isaiah consciously meant by the words does not matter. For Matthew, the Jewish scriptures were full of hints about the coming of Jesus: the fact that they were capable of bearing the interpretation he gave them was enough for them to be quoted. In adult life many of Jesus' actions were taken by the gospel writers to be a fulfilment of prophecy, and this introduces a new possibility, the fact that he did things deliberately to fulfil messianic expectations, as part of his undoubted awareness that at the very least he had been specially called by God.

THE SHEPHERDS' VISION
AT THE NATIVITY

LUKE ch2 vv1-20

WHEN angels appear in the Old Testament they do so in ancient stories which have developed over generations. It is sometimes hard to pin down the historical setting. The Garden of Eden is a primeval tale of origins produced by a society which had obviously no notion of evolution. Abraham and Moses are probably real people, and their stories have some plausibility in the context of what is known about the second millennium BC, but there is no external historical support for the details of their lives.

Jesus' birth took place as part of the intimate history of a family, but was recorded within living memory; at least some of his friends and relatives will have been alive when the gospels began to be written. The role played by the angels presents us with an acute historical challenge. This challenge is made clear by the second chapter of Luke. He begins by mentioning Augustus, well known as the founder of a dynasty of Roman emperors, who died in AD14. Quirinius, the governor of Syria, is also known from Roman records. It is known that at least one census took place during this time, and that the Herodian dynasty was dominant in Palestine. Luke fails to fix Jesus' birth accurately to the year, but he makes a good attempt when one considers that he will have lacked access to the kind of official records available to any modern historian. But then, within a few verses, we are presented with a host of angels appearing to a group of shepherds by night.

There is no point debating the plausibility of this event - the most that we can do is make some sense of it. There is a contrast

here: the angels are a host, that is, an army. They are the heavenly army, who in Jewish and early Christian speculation will ultimately defeat the forces of evil. In some Old Testament texts God is depicted as a king, with a heavenly court and an army, clearly a metaphor taken from political experience.

The angels announce the birth of a Messiah, an anointed king, in the city of David. It is no surprise that the shepherds are frightened. And yet, why are shepherds chosen to receive the announcement? And why does this mighty army speak of a baby born in humble circumstances, and end their proclamation with a message of peace? The contrast is surely deliberate. Luke wants us to understand that Jesus came first of all to redeem the outcasts, to throw in his lot with the despised, those on the margins of society. Shepherds were despised because they were poor and rootless, and due to their work unlikely to bother with the rigorous and precise demands of the Jewish law, of which the dominant Pharisaical party of the time made so much. Jesus is indeed a king, but a king born in an animal shelter, who would express his kingly power through humble compassion and the company not of good Jews, but both of Jews who had made a mess of their lives, and of unclean gentiles. He would establish the kingdom of God, not by destroying his enemies, but by inviting repentant sinners into it. The expected messianic banquet would take place not over the corpses of a conquered foe but in the context of the death of the king himself, a death which would be one pronounced accursed in the ancient texts of the Jewish law. But the story ends on a note of irony. As the shepherds come to Jesus to honour him, the Jewish reader will remember that once, long ago, Israel had been a shepherd people, guided by David, their shepherd-boy king.

THE FLIGHT INTO EGYPT

MATTHEW ch2 vv13-23

THE child Jesus is born into a world of powerful and hostile forces which are immediately ranged against him. His chances of survival are not good.

Once again, however, the angel of the Lord appears to Joseph in dreams. The forces of evil, represented by the dynasty of Herod, are outwitted at every point. The angel has already warned the magi to avoid him, and now Joseph leads his family into Egypt; even after Herod's death they settle in Nazareth to escape the clutches of his successor. The angel conveys the plans and purposes of God, and Joseph obeys without question. Herod is helpless, for his schemes are bound to be frustrated: how can a petty human tyrant compete with God himself? The story could easily have been given a comic flavour (and indeed in mediaeval mystery plays Herod is often treated as a comic villain), but for one important element. The purposes of God are never fulfilled without cost, and here one consequence of Herod's defeat is his massacre of the children in the region of Bethlehem, an event quite without a happy ending. In this way the reader is prepared for the shock of Jesus' own crucifixion at the end of the gospel.

It has already been made clear by Matthew that Jesus is a king in the line of David, born in David's city of Bethlehem. But he is also the new Moses. The massacre of the innocents recalls Pharaoh's massacre of the first-born. Matthew quotes Hosea's reference to the Israelite escape *from* Egypt in the context of Jesus' escape to Egypt: 'Out of Egypt have I called my son'. In that quotation God's son is Israel, and as the Messiah, Jesus represents the whole of Israel. The death of the children is connected to Jesus' own death, and they too represent suffering Israel: the quotation from Jeremiah about Rachel's tears in verse 18 refers to a legend that while the Jews were being deported to Babylon they passed Rachel's tomb at Ramah and the sound of weeping was heard coming from it. As Jacob's wife, Rachel was the matriarch of the twelve tribes of Israel.

The story is also given a firm historical basis. Herod may represent Pharaoh, but in history he was a client king at about the time of Jesus' birth. (He died in 4BC, so Luke is possibly mistaken in dating Jesus' birth to the governorship of Quirinius, which was around AD6). The angel appears to Joseph in dreams, so there is no difficulty over choirs of angels stretched across the sky. In fact, if angels really do exist, they may be encountered with equal plausibility in dreams or in mid-air, but their manifestation in the latter requires an effort of the imagination to believe. Appearances of angels can take many forms in many different kinds of environment.

There are of course those who argue that Matthew has constructed the whole story on the basis of Old Testament references, and it is true that he likes to support each important bit with a quotation, but unless he was following some genuine reminiscence of Jesus' earlier days, how would he have known which quotation to choose? The quotations do not always fit very well. In support of the memory that Jesus lived at Nazareth, Matthew quotes 'He shall be called a Nazoraean', which originally meant something quite different. The Old Testament reference is therefore subordinate to the memory of the real event. There is no other evidence for the massacre of the innocents, but the event is sadly credible. Herod was noted for his cruelty, and there is no reason to suppose that a comprehensive list of his atrocities was ever made. The numbers involved in the massacre may have been quite small, and Herod's reign produced quite enough royal murder victims from his own family to divert the attention of historians who wrote about him.

JESUS IS TEMPTED IN THE WILDERNESS

MATTHEW ch4 vv1-11

ANGELS do not turn up all over the place in the gospels, only on rare and significant occasions. The angel of the Lord appears at the beginning of Matthew to communicate with Joseph in dreams, and then again towards the end in the empty tomb to announce the Resurrection. These are not public occurrences, of the kind where someone might say, '*look, there's an angel*', and theoretically be able to record the event on film, but occurrences of an essentially mysterious and private kind (though none the less real for that), and they indicate some kind of communication from God to individuals and small groups. Matthew also mentions angels when speaking apocalyptically about the end of the world, but the end of the world is necessarily on the edge of recordable history, so the mention is appropriate. Angels are not necessarily servants of God; some are evil beings. Matthew mentions the devil and all his angels though it is not clear whether he thinks of these as inherently bad angels, or as good ones who rebelled.

Angels play a brief but important part in the Temptation story. The story is told in concrete terms, in that Jesus is in the wilderness and meets the devil who shows him various temptations. However, the story may also be understood as an internal struggle, as Jesus considers various ways in which he might work out his ministry, all of them false but superficially attractive avenues. Because they are false, they come from the fount of all deception, whatever that may be. There are various beliefs among Christians today about the existence of an actual being called the devil. Belief in the devil is

connected with beliefs about angels. If the devil is to be understood as a being who turned away from God in some primeval act of rebellion, then presumably angels have free will. If, on the other hand, angels are messengers programmed to do the work of God, then it makes no sense at all to imagine the devil as a fallen angel, because he would have had no free will with which to make his decision to rebel. People who do not believe in a personal devil are sometimes thought to be guilty of a foolish optimism about the world, but to deny the existence of the devil is not to deny the reality of a negative and chaotic power of human evil, accumulated and inherited down the millennia.

Jesus' temptations are all connected with the misuse of power to force a result, though the result sought is not necessarily a selfish one. The first temptation is still a temptation whoever is going to eat the bread.

He is also being tempted to test the power of God, to display a lack of trust. This is particularly important because his messiahship will be a way of suffering, not of power, and Jesus will have to preserve his trust in God even in the face of death. The devil suggests that angels will come to support Jesus 'lest you strike your foot against a stone' (Ps 91). The psalmist was writing a poem of trust in God's power and willingness to protect, and Jesus is being tempted to put this to the test, by throwing himself off the Temple.

This is in contrast to the deeds of power Jesus really did perform. Throwing himself off the Temple would have been an action quite without spiritual significance, a mere display. The miracles of the Messiah were of a quite different nature: the cures and exorcisms were a confrontation with evil, and look back to the messianic prophecies of Isaiah. Wherever Jesus works, Eden is restored. Madness and disease were seen by the ancient Jews as the work of evil spirits. Exorcism of evil spirits is still practised by some today; and for all, the different and various afflictions of insanity and disability can still plausibly be seen as evils, in the sense of being part of what is fundamentally wrong with the world. As for disease, if you try to define the 'evil spirits' supposed by the ancients to be its cause, any rough definition would also do for what are now called harmful bacteria and viruses - that is, invisible creatures operating in a way hostile to the human constitution.

What about the temptation to take the Kingdom by force? Some Jews were expecting a military Messiah, but the evangelist expresses the contradictory belief that all political power is in Satan's gift. Kings and rulers, as St Paul pointed out, keep the peace and punish criminals, and today there is a principle that political power should be maintained by consensus. But force is needed, and the ancients were aware that warfare, torture and execution are frequently part of the acquisition and maintenance of power. In the Old Testament, even as the Israelites demand a king after the anarchy of the time of the Judges, they are reminded that God is their king; these passages reflect a suspicion entertained towards all human claims to royal power. Jesus the Messiah must in any event resist the understandable temptation to force a solution by apparently quick and effective means. He is a king indeed, but not simply more powerful than earthly kings. His kingship is in a different style, a different mode, and its power works by hidden and unforeseen paths.

It is a paradox that simply because Jesus resists these temptations 'angels came and ministered to him' anyway. All the goods of this world, at which people grasp and clutch, will be given in surprising and unexpected ways by God to those who wait in love and trust: but the way to them is through death.

THE EMPTY TOMB

MATTHEW ch28 MARK ch16 LUKE ch24 JOHN ch20

THE empty tomb features in all four gospels. Jesus' followers come to visit his body after the crucifixion and find the tomb empty. They are confronted by figures, described as young men, or specified as angels, who assure them that Jesus is risen. No detailed description is given of these angels, except to say that they are dressed in white. This recalls the apocalyptic visions of the later parts of the Old Testament: white symbolises divine purity and the shining light of heaven. It is impossible to recapture exactly what was experienced by the first witnesses to the Resurrection, but the vision of angels is an appropriate feature. The gospels do not even attempt to describe the Resurrection itself: it is a meeting point between earth and heaven, and human description falters as the boundary of earthly things is reached.

Each gospel account contributes something to the indescribable truth of the whole event. In Matthew the *'angel of the Lord'* adopts a commanding role. The stone at the tomb is like the triumph of death, but, as he will at the last judgement, the angel comes from heaven, rolls away the stone, and sits on it. The guards lie like dead men, and Jesus has broken free. The angel communicates to the women his sure knowledge of what has happened and what it means. In their joy the women are filled with energy, they run to tell their news, and the pace of the narrative matches theirs. The witness of women was not admissible in Jewish law, being deemed unreliable, and it is significant that they are chosen as bearers of this most important message, for God is not bound by the prejudices of human society.

Mark is more restrained in his account and, as ever, this makes him more mysterious. Inside the tomb the women meet a 'young man' sitting on the right hand side, who announces to them that Jesus is risen, telling them to pass the message on to the disciples. But they are terrified, and flee without telling anyone. It seems that the original text of Mark ends at this point and no resurrection appearances are mentioned: the followers of Christ must put their faith in the empty tomb and the words of a mysterious angelic youth.

Luke's version has two young men dressed in dazzling clothes, who explain to the women that the Resurrection makes sense of Jesus' earlier predictions. This angelic authentication is called into question when the disciples pour scorn on the women's testimony, and Peter visits the tomb. It is indeed empty, but the young men have gone. In Luke it is only when Jesus appears to his disciples that they realise he is risen. There is a contrast here between the calm assurance of the angelic figures and the confused incredulity of Jesus' disciples. They cannot believe the witness of mere women, joining the ranks of those Old Testament figures who refused to believe the words of angels.

In John too, the first witness to the Resurrection is a woman, but the male followers of Jesus are depicted in a less foolish light. Two parallel processes happen. Mary tells Peter and the Beloved Disciple that someone has taken the body of Jesus (the common-sense explanation of the empty tomb), but the sight of the grave clothes neatly folded convinces them that Jesus is risen. Mary, still in confusion, is reassured by two angels, who ask her why she is weeping. The gentleness of the angels' question is a contrast to the declamatory tone of the angels in the other gospels, and prepares the way for the beautifully related encounter between Mary and the risen Jesus, whom she at first mistakes for the gardener. Just as long ago when the first sin was committed God walked in the garden he had made, so now the Word of God himself appears in the garden where sin and death have been swallowed up in his glorious resurrection.

THE ASCENSION

ACTS ch1 vv9-11

LUKE begins the Acts of the Apostles with an account of the Ascension of Jesus. Angels are used to explain the event to the disciples, and to rebuke them for misunderstanding it. The rebuke is somewhat stylised, and hardly a condemnation. Throughout the gospels the disciples are rebuked for failing to understand some aspect of Jesus' significance or teaching, and their failure is a very human one in which we all share. They are slow to pick up the message of some of Jesus' more difficult parables, find it hard to come to terms with Jesus' predictions of his resurrection, and none of this is surprising.

The Acts of the Apostles is on the surface a straightforward treatment of early Christianity, and our hopes are raised when the author identifies himself as the same person who wrote the gospel of Luke and addresses the same reader Theophilus. However, though he reminds Theophilus of the content of the gospel, he fails to introduce his new book, which rather oddly begins with an ending, the disappearance of Jesus from daily discourse with his followers. As you read on, you realise that the title traditionally given to the book is misleading: the only apostles given prominent treatment are first Peter and then Paul, and the whole thing ends not with Paul's death but with his arrival at Rome.

The Ascension itself is difficult to understand. It is described in naively pictorial terms: Jesus goes up to heaven in a cloud, and his disciples stand looking upwards. What are we to make of this? One might want to say that the early Christians lived in a pre-scientific age and thought that God lived in the sky. Jesus was returning to

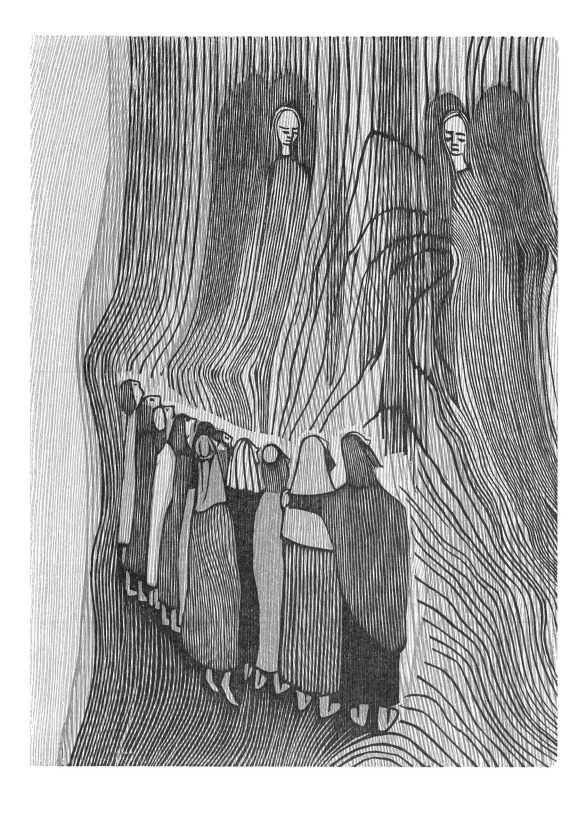

God and therefore is imagined as floating up into the air. But this approach fails to do justice to the sophistication and depth of pre-scientific religious belief, as if the spirituality of first century Judaism were to be equated with the cargo cults practised by the tribesmen of Papua New Guinea in our own time. In fact the angels rebuke the disciples for standing looking up into the sky. The central truth of the Ascension does not lie in the subjective experience of the disciples - what they actually saw - but in the fact that some time after his resurrection Jesus ceased to be visibly discernible in our own dimension and was once more with God. He would continue to work in the world through his spirit, and that work is what Acts is all about, and that is why it begins with an ending.

As so often in the Bible, when human characters experience the presence of God, coded language is used to point to something which cannot be captured by normal human language. Here Jesus is returning to a 'higher' order of existence, so he is seen as vanishing into the sky. The cloud, as in the Exodus, reveals God, but reveals him as hidden and mysterious. The angels are strangely prosaic: they simply arrive as men in white beside the disciples and deliver their message, defined, like all angels, by their function as explaining and interpreting the ways of heaven.

What must it have been like to witness the Ascension of Jesus? We can no longer know, and the only access we can have is through the coded language given to us by the evangelist.

THE APOSTLES ARE RELEASED
FROM PRISON

ACTS ch5 vv17-19 & ch12 vv6-11

LUKE says that the High Priest's party, the Sadducees, arrested the apostles out of jealousy. The apostles had been healing people in the power of the Spirit: so great was their reputation that the sick were being laid in their shadow as they passed by. Not surprising then that the ruling faction of Judaism, old fashioned and trading on its aristocratic and priestly status, should feel threatened and throw the apostles into prison. It had engineered the death of Jesus the false prophet, but his ghost would not lie still. The Sadducees have at their disposal all the mechanisms of human power and authority: prison, to contain and silence the subversives, and scourges to frighten them into obedience.

The power of God works in a different way. The angel of the Lord comes to release the apostles, but not with any dramatic display of strength. The power of God is quiet, and at first unnoticed by the human authorities: the apostles have gone, but the prison gates are still locked. The powers of the world and the power of God do not compete on the level with a trial of equivalent strength. It is not a question of the hosts of heaven having more divisions than the armies of earthly powers. The Sadducees can continue to flog and imprison, and even after their mysterious release by the angel, the apostles are still hauled before the council and interrogated. We know that the empires of the world will continue to bind and enforce and will finally be able to destroy the earth. The apostles themselves will continue to be hounded, and many of them will suffer death in terrible forms. But what can all the powers of earth do against a God who can simply choose to ignore the constraints of prison, to rearrange the prison gates by altering the configuration of the atoms he himself has created? The power of this God is ultimately subversive against all forms of human power, it mocks them by ignoring them and following its own course.

When the council finally meets, the Sadducees want to kill the apostles as they killed Jesus. The gospel accounts talked of blasphemy as the charge in that case, but it was hardly blasphemous to be a Messiah: many Jews were waiting for one. What the Sadducees could not tolerate was that God had confounded their expectations by sending as Messiah someone they did not want, so they called him a false prophet and rejected his message. As men of power, their solution was death.

Here however, the apostles are saved for the time being by help from a surprising quarter: a famous Pharisee, Gamaliel. Though fierce opponents of Jesus, the Pharisees were more spiritually adept than the Sadducees. They sought to live righteously by the detailed precepts of the Law, meditated on the names of angels, and yearned for the resurrection of the dead. Many seem to have followed Paul's example in converting to the new way. Gamaliel warns the council to let the apostles go free. If they are preaching a false messiah, their movement will vanish in time, otherwise the council may find itself challenging the power of God himself. In view of the casual way in which the angel released the apostles from prison, his words are wise indeed.

The story of Peter's release from prison is very different, though it too involves an angel of the Lord, and deals with an attempt to suppress the new movement of the followers of the way of Jesus.

This time the villain is Herod, though it is not clear which one: various members of the dynasty bore the name, and the most likely candidate is Herod Antipas, the one who executed John the Baptist and interrogated Jesus. Once again the conflict is between two powers, but this time the power of God brings swift and terrible results. This Herod lacks the excuse of allegiance to a religious tradition: as a half-foreign king sponsored by Rome he is simply trying to curry favour with the Jewish authorities. The treatment of the theme is detailed and literary: we start with Herod initiating a persecution against the followers of Jesus, and end with the king suffering a wretched punishment for blasphemy. Here we have the popular belief in earthly retribution for sin, and Luke seems to have succumbed to the temptation of regarding a tyrant's death from an unpleasant disease as a sign of God's vengeance. Herod the Great, who founded the dynasty, had died in a similar way, and at the beginning of Acts, Luke departs from the Matthaean tradition of Judas' suicide and thinks that Judas died accidently in a field bought with the blood money: another fitting end.

Between the two references to Herod comes the central part of the story in which Peter's encounter with the angel is told in detail: the angel brings light, the chains fall away and the gates swing open. Peter's experience is realistically told: he assumes he is dreaming or seeing a vision until he finds himself alone in the street, the angel having left him. His friends are slow to believe that he has been released, and imagine at first that the apparition at their door is his 'angel'. This presumably means some sort of genius or guardian angel, and there was obviously a curious belief that our guardian angels resemble us in appearance, are our doubles, as it were.

This belief has no spiritual function to perform in the story, but is one of the aspects which bring it to life. It is easy to picture the events unfolding, which is strange, as they are centred on the miraculous, but the human responses are plausible and naturalistically related. Having announced himself to his friends, Peter mysteriously departs to another place, on some unspecified business. The unfortunate prison guards, having been examined by Herod, are killed: an act of casual cruelty of a kind for which his family were famous.

MINISTERING ANGELS

HEBREWS ch1 vv5-14

THE letter to the Hebrews is a strange piece. The addressees are as anonymous as the author. The people of the Old Testament had not been called Hebrews since the time of the captivity in Egypt, and it is not clear why the name is revived here. However, the letter is valuable for its early Christian understanding of Jesus' work, and in particular, the function performed by angels in the divine plan.

Angels operate as intermediaries between God and humans. They help to inhibit an anthropomorphic picture of God: in early texts humans are represented as walking and talking with God directly, but in later ones they more frequently communicate via an angel sent from God, and the angel can safely be imagined as a human figure, or at least a voice. For Christians, who continued to believe in angels, there was a problem: Jesus had come to be understood as God in human form, as the final communication or Word from God: seeing Jesus is seeing the Father. Did this mean that Jesus was a sort of angel? If not, what function were angels now to perform?

It is not clear how far along the path to an understanding of Jesus as God-become-man the writer to Hebrews had gone. The letter's date is uncertain: it is full of profound Christian reflection, suggesting a later date, and yet it seems to assume that the Temple at Jerusalem is still standing, and the Temple was destroyed in AD70. The writer elevates Jesus to a unique position, higher than the angels. He is God's heir, the agent of creation who upholds the universe, and in his own nature he is 'stamped' with the nature of

God. He reflects God's glory. Yet strangely, and characteristically of some very early Christian thought, he seems to have achieved or have been given this status, rather than having had it since eternity. (The prologue to John's gospel is much more clear about fixing Jesus' status as eternal Word from the beginning). The writer to Hebrews uses a collection of Old Testament texts, and fills them with new meaning: an old royal psalm is adapted to represent Jesus as God's Son, but not a mere adopted son like an Israelite king.

No angel has been given this privilege. The angels are only servants of God: they fall down and worship the Son. Their nature and appearance are changeable at God's decree, they can be wind or flames of fire, whereas by implication, Jesus' humanity is a fixed part of his identity. And where do these angels stand in the hierarchy of creation? They come *down* from heaven, and reflect the power of God in their dealings with humans, but this passage makes it clear that they are there to serve humanity, assisting the Son in the work of salvation. One possibility is to suppose that angels are close to God in that they automatically reflect his will, while lacking the freedom of choice which offers to humans a unique glory but also a terrible risk. However, some have thought that angels too have this freedom: Satan was an angel who fell, and his rebellion blighted the world at the very moment of its creation, but the writer to Hebrews shows no awareness of this story.

ANGELS AS MESSENGERS

REVELATION chs8 - 10

THESE chapters form part of a vision of the end of the world. The style of writing is apocalyptic, that is, to do with heavenly secrets being revealed to the chosen by a prophet or seer. The imagery tends to be rich and violent, and the predictions may be applied either to some near contemporary event like a Roman defeat - to which a writer may want to allude with due discretion - or to the end of the world, which may have to be described in vague and conventional terms. For the imagery of apocalyptic writing does tend to be conventional, involving standard references to cosmic upheavals, angels and heavenly beasts, significant numbers and the like, and can be used to refer to a variety of contemporary or future occurrences.

The book of Revelation is often attacked for the relish with which it describes the sufferings of the damned and the destruction of the earth. But it must be remembered that the writer is a member of a persecuted minority which seems to have believed that the world was in the grip of an evil empire, and that at a deeper level it had been given over to the powers of darkness. (Why else would the devil have been able to offer the world to Jesus?) If in the last days it is to be returned to the power of the God who created it, there will necessarily be enormous upheaval and great suffering.

The seven angels in these passages blow their trumpets to announce a new order. Their actions are stylised and liturgical - another angel carries a censer - and they unleash terrible plagues, recalling the punishments threatened by God on Israel and inflicted on the Egyptians. More angels are introduced, and described using the kind of divine imagery hard to depict: we have an angel wrapped in a cloud with a rainbow over his head, his face like the sun and his legs like pillars of fire: though hard to depict, the language is familiar in the Bible from Exodus onwards. Abbadon/Apollyon is mentioned as the angel of the underworld and king of the giant locusts: he is not to be identified with Satan, but with the angel of death and destruction, who carries out the purposes of God.

The intention seems to be to goad the pagan nations of the world into repentance, but they stay fixed in their evil ways. The writer is not here showing culpable intolerance of another religion: he clearly believed that pagans worshipped demons and were therefore siding with the devil against the true interests of humanity. They were also persecuting - so far quite effectively - the followers of Jesus. Four murderous angels are released from the river Euphrates to cause havoc and destruction: at this time, the Roman empire itself lived in dread of attack from the Parthians, an Asian people who like the scorpions in this passage could sting from behind, in that their mounted archers would turn and shoot salvoes of arrows as they galloped away in retreat.

Only with devastation such as this could there be any hope of divine vindication at the end of time. What terrible experiences of persecution must there have been to call forth from this writer such yearning for such a catastrophe?

FINAL WARNING OF JUDGEMENT

REVELATION ch14 vv6-13

THIS is one of the most notorious passages in the book of Revelation. It is a source for belief in the eternal punishment of the damned. Jesus himself taught that a permanent rejection of God would lead to destruction, but it seems that belief in resurrection to eternal bliss predated belief in eternal damnation. The persecuted brothers in the second book of Maccabees hope for resurrection for themselves, but tell the wicked king that he will remain dead. However by the time of Jesus, popular Jewish religious consciousness was more familiar with the idea of eternal punishment for the wicked. It forms the background to the parable of the rich man and Lazarus in Luke's gospel. In Revelation there is an unpleasantly judicial flavour to the proceedings. The Lamb (Jesus) and his heavenly court will watch while the damned, the worshippers of the Beast, are everlastingly tortured with fire. Is this spectacle going to be one of the joys of heaven?

It is a partial answer to say that the writer of Revelation is talking about the punishment of servants of the Beast, and the Beast stands for the persecuting Roman empire, which treated Christians with the utmost cruelty: we should not be glib about enjoining forgiveness on those whose sufferings we have not shared. But the writer does seem to be succumbing to a desire for vengeance quite out of keeping with the spirit of the gospel.

He is surely imagining a turning of the tables in which the courtroom brutality of ancient Rome is visited on Roman officials who tortured Christians. Even if we have a problem with the images used, justice does demand that in some way the balance

should be redressed, that in some final reckoning all the terrible cruelties inflicted on the innocent and righteous should be overturned. Evil must not have the last word. Even if, with many Christians today, we believe that everyone will ultimately be saved, this must involve a facing up to what has been done, and an acknowledgement of the cost of forgiveness.

Perhaps we are also forgetting that this is apocalyptic. We may not like the writer using the imagery of judicial torture, but it may be that we should not take it any more literally than the description it follows of the servants of the Beast being made to drink the cup of God's wrath, an Old Testament metaphor of obscure significance. The choice of image does however reveal an attitude of mind which is satisfied with only a limited view of God's mercy and justice, and modern Christian readers do not have to regard the choice as directly inspired by the Holy Spirit, any more than they have to believe that God accepts slavery as an institution just because the New Testament does. There is more to the mystery of good and evil than God being revealed as a Roman emperor on a grand scale, waiting to punish his rebellious subjects.

WAR IN HEAVEN

REVELATION ch12 vv1-17

IN Paradise Lost, Satan rebels at the beginning of time before the creation of the world. He and his fellow rebel angels declare war on God. He is vanquished, and his fall causes the subsequent fall of man. In Revelation, the writer imagines the fall taking place just before the end of the world, and that the sufferings of the righteous are being caused by the defeated devil falling to earth and oppressing them for a time before his final condemnation. The theme of a heavenly struggle between good and evil is found in more than one religion, but here it is made clear that God and Satan are not two equal principles. Satan can do nothing without God's permission - he can only stay on earth for a short time - and he battles not with God himself but with Michael, the leader of the angels of God. Ever since this passage, Michael has been imagined as a mighty warrior spearing Satan with his lance, and Milton sees him as a general under God's command.

This chapter in Revelation is not describing events in linear time. It begins with a portent, supposedly referring to a future occurrence, but the portent looks very like the conception and birth of Jesus, transferred to a heavenly dimension. The times are symbolic, and it is made clear that various images can be used to describe the devil, the eternal adversary of humankind: fallen angel, serpent or dragon.

The passage may be intended to conjure up a variety of impressions in the mind of the reader. Some commentators suggest that there is a link with the myth of Apollo's birth to Leto and his struggle with the serpent Pytho. Not only was Apollo a uniquely powerful god, but the emperor Nero claimed identity with him. Nero was a persecuting emperor who was supposed to have been divine, and one of the issues of the early persecutions was competition between the lordship of Christ and Caesar. But we do not need to go to pagan models for this picture. In the Old Testament there are echoes of even more ancient myths from Mesopotamia. A serpent or dragon which variously encircles the earth, or dwells in the watery chaos, threatens to engulf the world and upset the plans of the gods who bring harmony and order. Here, at the end of the chapter the dragon goes off to make war on the offspring of the woman, reminding us of the garden of Eden and the prophecy of enmity between the serpent and the children of Eve. From an early date the Virgin Mary was regarded as the new Eve, and she came to be represented in art as crowned with stars and standing on the moon, like the woman in this passage.

And so we end as we began, with the Book of Genesis and the angels in the guise of mythological beasts. There the cherubim stood with drawn swords to protect frail humans from the full consequences of their sin. Here all the angels are ranged together in a great myth of conflict, the war in heaven. Although this passage comes early in the Book of Revelation, it looks to the end as well as to the beginning of time; the war has echoes down the ages in the form of our own daily struggle with evil, with a resonance as pervasive as the surviving noise of that great primeval explosion by which God brought the universe into existence.

EPILOGUE

THIS has been a treatment in words and pictures of selected biblical passages in which angels are encountered. There is a subjectivity about it, as about the experiences themselves, and yet perhaps some inkling of what angels might be has been given.

Many more passages could have been selected, and the question may be asked why so many people met angels in biblical times and not today. It may be that the world has grown too sophisticated for angels, that the advances of technology have made them seem a quaint survival from a more primitive age. Or conversely, the world may have grown dull and lost any sensitivity to their presence.

It might be pointed out that the Bible covers a long period of history, from about 1800BC (a possible date for Abraham) to AD100 (a possible date for the book of Revelation). Over this range the writers have concentrated on events and experiences of spiritual significance. In the early chapters of Genesis, before the appearance of Abraham, they extend their perspective backwards into a universal prehistory, relying on traditional stories rather than memories of particular people and events. The scope of the Bible is such that its concentration on religious experiences is entirely understandable. Even within the historical period, some of the books of the Bible contain more history than others: the Book of Tobit is a good example of a romance placed within a plausible historical setting. The fact that angels appear in sub-historical books as well as historical ones is a poor argument against the possibility of genuine appearances. Witches are a modern example of figures appearing both in fairy tales and in real life, though various assessments can be made of their actual powers.

Angels continue to appear in the Bible even after the coming of

Jesus, though their significance begins to change. Throughout subsequent history they have been met at various times, though not always recognised as such. Each alleged appearance should be discussed on its merits. To take one example, the angel of Mons, which is supposed to have appeared to the British army in 1914, was not seen by every soldier. There are various possible explanations for what was seen, but a genuine apparition should not be ruled out from the start.

However, in our present age of privatised religion with the emphasis laid on personal journeys in faith, (notwithstanding the ever present challenge of what used to be called the social gospel), experiences of angels have tended to be unashamedly subjective: strange meetings, the awareness of whose significance may be confined to those having them, and which may appear to others as a matter of coincidence.

As a new millennium approaches there may well be an increase in angelic apparitions, explain them how you will, but I doubt if these will be as dramatically public as they are imagined as being in the book of Revelation. The appearance of an angel need create no stir at all, and it is no surprise that a generation whose imagination is largely confined to its own species should most frequently come across angels in the guise of humans. In this they would do well to heed the advice given by the writer of Hebrews, advice particularly appropriate for this generation: *'Do not neglect to show hospitality to strangers, for thereby some have entertained angels unawares.'*